Mastery Rewards Patience

A Trader's Journey

By

Joël Pérodin

Mastery Rewards Patience: A Trader's Journey

This book is intended for informational and educational purposes only. It does not guarantee profit or financial success, and it should not be interpreted as financial advice. Trading involves risk. Always perform your own due diligence.

ISBN: *979-8-2954-1529-6*
Cover & Interior Design: Joël Pérodin
First Edition
Printed in the United States of America.

For inquiries or permissions, email:
jperenterprises@gmail.com

Dedication

To those who walk beside me, grounding me with clarity, purpose, and a kind of patience I didn't know lived within me.
To the ones whose strength, sacrifice, and quiet guidance shaped my resilience and work ethic—your influence is woven into every page of this book.
To the silent supporters who stood with me in the moments that mattered most, offering strength in ways words rarely capture.
And to everyone who believed in me even when the path ahead wasn't clear—your faith, support, and prayers carried me farther than you know.

This book exists because I refused to quit, and because you gave me reasons not to.

About the Author

Joël Pérodin is a photographer, music producer, entrepreneur, and trader based in the Washington D.C.–Maryland–Virginia area. His creative background began long before he ever looked at a price chart. Through photography and music, he learned rhythm, timing, light, and emotion—skills that would later influence the way he viewed the markets.

Joël's trading journey began with a simple curiosity: *Why do so many people fear the market?* What started as interest quickly grew into a seven-year pursuit of understanding, discipline, and self-mastery. Trading revealed parts of himself he didn't know existed—impatience, doubt, resilience, awareness—and forced him to confront them directly.

Without traders in his immediate circle, he navigated the highs and lows with self-taught discipline and unshakable persistence. Those quiet years shaped his philosophy: that true mastery begins within, and that the market is only a mirror reflecting the trader's internal world.

Beyond trading, Joël is a devoted partner to Sergine and a proud father to his daughter, Thalia. Fatherhood deepened his commitment to patience, clarity, and purpose—values that shape every chapter of this book. His entrepreneurial spirit carries across multiple ventures, each driven by creativity, discipline, and a desire to inspire others.

Through *Mastery Rewards Patience*, Joël shares the lessons that took him years to internalize. His hope is simple: to help traders discover the version of themselves capable of long-term consistency, emotional discipline, and calm execution.

To connect with Joël, ask questions, or inquire about hands-on trading guidance, you can reach him at:
jperenterprises@gmail.com

How to Read This Book

Trading is not a skill you learn once. It's an evolving practice shaped by your patience, your identity, and your discipline.
This book is designed to guide you through both **who you must become** and **how you must operate** to trade with calm consistency.

There are **two phases** — and you should not rush through either one.

Phase One: Mindset & Growth

Phase One builds the psychological foundation you need to trade with clarity.
These chapters are not about charts—they are about **you**.

You will learn:

- how to wait without stress
- how to reset after setbacks
- how to understand your emotional patterns
- how structure protects your sanity
- how resilience is built quietly over time

Read Phase One slowly.
Pause after each chapter.
Journal your thoughts, frustrations, patterns, and breakthroughs.
This phase transforms confusion into clarity and chaos into discipline.

If you rush here, trading will always feel hard.

Phase Two: Strategy & Execution

Phase Two translates your emotional mastery into mechanical rules.

This section teaches:

- candlesticks as price language
- market structure
- ATR and volatility windows
- volume conviction
- the ORB strategy
- session rhythms
- prop-firm execution
- multi-account scaling

- journaling + expectancy

Study Phase Two like a technician.
Have charts open.
Practice in simulation.
Review examples slowly and deliberately.

If Phase One is who you become, Phase Two is how you operate.

You cannot skip one and expect mastery.

Your Reading Rhythm

Here's how to move through the book:

Phase One:
Read 1–2 chapters at a time.
Reflect.
Journal.
Build awareness.

Phase Two:
Study with charts.
Mark examples.
Apply in sim.
Repeat until mechanical.

Every future breakthrough you have will come from respecting both phases equally—**inner discipline and outer execution**.

A Final Note Before You Begin

This is not a book about trading tricks or shortcuts. This is a guide to mastering yourself **through** trading.

When you finish both phases, you will not only trade better—you will think better, decide better, and live calmer.

Mastery rewards the trader who stays.

Table of Contents

Mastery Rewards Patience: A Trader's Journey

Phase One — Mindset & Growth

Phase Two — Strategy & Execution

Author's Note (My Journey)

I didn't grow up around charts or finance. I grew up around rhythm. Music, photography, light, and timing were my teachers long before the market ever was. When I first opened a trading platform, I didn't see numbers—I saw tempo. Patterns that pulsed and breathed. And I thought, if I can learn this rhythm, I can master it.

I was never chasing money. I was chasing understanding.
Why did people fear the market so much?
Why did calm decision-making seem so rare?

Seven years later, the answer revealed itself: people weren't afraid of the market. They were afraid of themselves. The market only amplifies what is already inside—impatience, greed, hesitation, ego. Every candle exposes a truth we try to hide.

Trading taught me more about myself than any book or mentor ever could. It revealed how emotion slips into logic, how silence can feel heavier than loss, and how real growth happens in moments no one else sees. I used to think consistency meant never losing. Now I know it means never breaking process.

If those who love me knew how much I spent on trading—how much I lost—they would have called me crazy. Over seven years, I burned through thousands of dollars, not out of greed, but obsession. The need to figure it out. I kept quiet because no one around me traded. I had no one to talk to, no one who understood the invisible war inside every click of buy or sell.

It is a lonely path.
The isolation hurts more than the losses.

Everyone sees trading as gambling until they see what it reveals about a person. I always believed some of the people around me could have done better than me—they simply never tried. But none of that matters unless you step into the arena.

Trading isn't about money. It's about discovering who you are when no one is cheering for you. The truth is simple:

You don't trade charts.
You trade your own psychology.

This book is the story of learning that truth the hard way.

A reflection on isolation, self-discovery, and the quiet persistence required for true trading mastery.

Phase One

Mindset and Growth

Chapter 1 - The Invisible Battle

Every trader fights two markets: the external one made of prices and candles, and the internal one made of emotions and impulses. When I began, I believed I was battling volatility. Over time I discovered the truth—what I was really battling were my reactions to it.

The invisible battle does not start on the chart; it begins the moment you open your platform and your mind floods with possibility, fear, and endless what-ifs. A single move on the screen can spark an entire story in your head about what you "could have made" or "should have caught." That isn't strategy. That is survival mode disguised as analysis.

I once believed discipline meant not feeling emotions at all. Now I understand discipline means feeling everything, but choosing structure over impulse. Patience is forged in the space between urge and restraint. Each time you override the impulse to act recklessly, you win a small, invisible victory—one that compounds into trust.

The inner battle never disappears. It only changes shape.
Sometimes it whispers, "Take one more trade."
Other times, "Double size to make it back."
Every rushed decision is a vote for chaos. Chaos doesn't need many votes to take control.

With experience, I learned to prepare for this battle before the first candle even forms. It starts with calm—journaling my mood, checking my emotional state, and deciding if I'm fit to trade. If I'm tired, angry, or distracted, I step away. The market rewards clarity, not courage.

Some days the bravest move is closing the charts early and admitting, "Today isn't the day." That isn't a weakness. It is maturity.

The more respect you give your state of mind, the more consistent your results become.
In the end, the hardest part of trading isn't the market itself—it is staying centered while it moves.

A reflection on how awareness transforms discipline into lasting calm.

Chapter 2 - Shortcuts Steal Substance

When I look back on my early trading years, I see a pattern—not on the charts, but within myself. Every time I tried to skip a step, I ended up paying double later. Each shortcut promised less pain and faster progress, yet it only postponed the lesson waiting for me.

I chased every new indicator, every one-click strategy, convinced there was a hidden edge that would make trading easy. What I really wanted was progress without discomfort. Reward without repetition. But the market taught me something simple: if you didn't earn it, you can't keep it.

Shortcuts feel exciting because they hide the friction of growth. They create the illusion of speed—the illusion that the next tweak or tool might finally solve everything. But mastery doesn't come from tweaking. It grows from repetition. The repetition that feels boring is the repetition that shapes precision.

In trading, feedback appears whether you want it or not. When you rush, the same lesson reappears again and again, patiently waiting for you to slow down and learn it. Fast results fade because they rest on borrowed understanding. Real progress is earned, not downloaded.

I learned that patience isn't just waiting for setups. It's earning conviction through data, journaling, and honest reflection. Each time I reviewed my trades and confronted my patterns, I moved closer to the trader I wanted to become. There is no shortcut to that kind of awareness. And awareness is the only edge that never decays.

Shortcuts may give speed, but they steal substance.

You might win a few trades by getting lucky, but luck doesn't scale. If your skills don't match your ambition, the market exposes you. Every rushed decision—breaking a rule, forcing a trade, skipping confirmation—is a seed that grows into future losses.

Eventually, I realized shortcuts weren't saving me time. They were stealing my future. I didn't need a new strategy. I needed a new mindset. Once I stopped trying to outsmart the process, the process began to work for me. Entries became calmer. Losses became educational. Wins became steady. My trading shifted from a chase into a partnership.

Patience isn't waiting. Patience is trust—trust that the long path is the real path, and the only path that leads anywhere worth going.

Shortcuts promise speed, but repetition builds mastery.

A reflection on how rushing sacrifices foundation, while disciplined repetition creates lasting growth.

Chapter 3 - The Discipline of Waiting

Waiting once felt like a punishment. In my early days of trading, the silence on the chart was unbearable—an emptiness I tried to fill with action. I would scroll through timeframes, hunting for something to justify a trade. Deep down, I wasn't looking for opportunity. I was trying to escape the discomfort of stillness. What I didn't understand was that impatience wasn't caused by a lack of setups; it was caused by a lack of trust—trust in my system, trust in my preparation, and trust in myself.

Over time, I learned that patience isn't passive. It's not doing nothing. It's the deliberate choice to wait without letting restlessness take control. There is a quiet discipline in waiting that no one celebrates, yet it is one of the most powerful skills a trader can develop. No one applauds the trades you didn't take. But those moments—the ones where you sit on your hands—are the ones that protect your capital and strengthen your identity.

The best setups rarely scream for attention. They form quietly, almost calmly, as if the market is preparing a moment of clarity for those willing to watch. Rushing that process blinds you. You don't see structure forming. You don't see imbalance building. You only see motion—and you mistake that motion for opportunity.

I began to recognize a dangerous moment just before breaking my rules: the moment when my mind whispered, "Maybe this one will work." That wasn't intuition. It was impatience wearing hope like a mask. By learning to recognize that voice, I learned to pause. That pause became a habit. That habit became discipline. And that discipline saved me from countless unnecessary losses.

With time, waiting became something else entirely. It became an act of respect—respect for my rules, my plan, and my future. Every time I waited for true alignment, I proved to myself that I was capable of restraint. That tiny victory compounded into confidence.

The market is not my opponent during these moments—it is my mirror. When nothing is happening, it's showing me who I am when no one is watching. Am I calm, or am I desperate? Am I patient, or am I bored? Am I disciplined, or am I drifting?

These days, when I wait, I wait with purpose. Not out of fear. Not out of hesitation. But because I know the difference between noise and opportunity. Waiting is preparation. Waiting is clarity building. Waiting is the foundation of every clean execution that follows.

Waiting is not wasting time. Waiting is sharpening timing.

MASTERY REWARDS PATIENCE

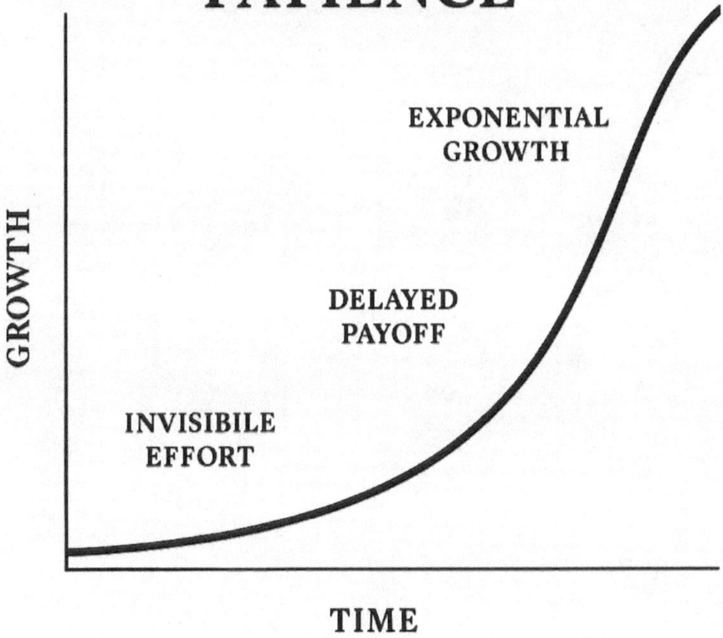

Chapter 4 - How I Learned to Be Patient (Constantly)

Patience was never something I chose because I wanted to. It was something I learned because the market gave me no other option. The market doesn't respond to your urgency or make exceptions for your excitement. It does not care how badly you want a setup. It moves on its own time, and if you try to rush it, it teaches you the cost—every single time.

In the beginning, I stared at charts for hours, taking trades simply because price moved. Movement felt like opportunity, and silence felt like a trap. The result was predictable: I overtraded, forced entries, and paid for every moment of impatience. The losses hurt, but what hurt more was the feeling that I had betrayed my own plan. Not the drawdown in the account, but the drawdown in my self-trust.

With time, I realized patience wasn't a mood—it was a muscle. And like any muscle, it needed repetition to grow stronger. So I simplified everything. One trade per session. No market orders. No revenge trades. No exceptions. These weren't advanced techniques. They were boundaries—anchors in the fog.

I began tracking something new: not just my results, but how often I broke my rules. That simple act changed everything. Instead of measuring myself by wins or losses, I measured myself by behavior. Every time I resisted the urge to act without confirmation, I gained a piece of the discipline I lacked before.

Those small moments—those micro-reps of patience—became the foundation of my trading. Days with no trades stopped feeling like missed opportunities. They felt like victories. They were proof that I could wait for a setup instead of chasing one. Slowly, the noise faded, and the clarity increased.

Patience also followed me outside the charts. I started noticing how often I rushed conversations, rushed decisions, rushed my own thoughts. The same muscle that helped me wait for a clean setup helped me become calmer in my life. I wasn't reacting to everything anymore. I was responding with intention.

The truth is, patience cannot be built in one dramatic moment. It is built in the smallest decisions—choosing to hold steady when everything in you wants to act. Choosing to wait one more minute. Choosing to trust that your preparation is stronger than your impulses.

Every delayed impulse becomes a step toward mastery. Every moment of waiting becomes part of your identity. And after enough repetition, something powerful happens: you stop fighting the market's rhythm and start syncing with it.

Patience isn't a trait. It's a skill. And like all skills, it grows through practice, not hope.

A reflection on how steady, consistent restraint transforms impatience into clarity, and waiting into strength.

Chapter 5 - Where Patience Ends and Action Begins

Patience is powerful—but only when it leads to action. For a long time, I confused hesitation with discipline. I held back on perfect setups, telling myself I was "waiting for more confirmation." In reality, I was afraid to execute. I was hiding my fear behind the appearance of patience.

There is a fine line between patience and paralysis. Patience prepares you. Paralysis protects your fear. The market doesn't reward waiting forever. It rewards decisive action born from real preparation.

There came a moment in my journey when I realized I couldn't become a confident trader without proof. Proof only comes from action. You don't build trust in your system by thinking about it—you build trust by executing it. One clean trade builds more confidence than a week of analysis.

To solve this, I created what I call "commitment cues"—clear conditions that tell me it is time to act. ATR meets the threshold. The opening range is clean. Volume is rising. Structure aligns. Three confirmations, no hesitation. When those boxes are checked, the decision is already made. My job is simply to execute.

The more I trusted my preparation, the less I feared the trigger. Execution became the natural conclusion of patience, not the enemy of it. I learned that perfection never appears on a chart. If you wait for a "perfect setup," you will wait your whole trading career. There's no perfection—only readiness.

Patience is meant to lead to execution, not endless waiting. The silence before a setup is not a sign to doubt—it is a sign to prepare. When the signal appears, hesitation only weakens the opportunity. The cleanest trades come from clarity, and clarity comes from knowing exactly when patience must end and action must begin.

Now, when I see my criteria align, I don't negotiate with myself. I follow my plan. I act once, act clean, and let the market do the rest. After entering, patience takes over again—this time to let the trade play out without interference.

In this balance of waiting and acting, mastery takes shape. Patience finds its purpose, and execution gains its strength.

Patience is preparation. Execution is commitment. Mastery requires both.

Chapter 6 - The Curve of Mastery

For years, I thought I wasn't progressing. I studied, journaled, refined my setups, and still felt stuck. My growth looked flat—no consistent wins, no breakthrough, no upward curve. What I didn't realize then is that mastery never grows in a straight line. It grows in long, quiet stretches before it rises sharply.

That flat part of the curve is where most traders quit. It's uncomfortable because it feels like the effort isn't working. You show up every day, follow the rules, protect your capital—and yet nothing seems to change. But that phase is not failure. It is preparation. It is the root system forming underground before anything blooms above the surface.

Mastery grows silently. Every skipped bad trade, every clean ORB execution, every journal entry, every patient session when you chose the plan over emotion—those moments compound even when you can't see the results yet. Over time, they build a foundation that can finally support real growth.

The breakthrough always feels sudden, but it never is. It's the accumulation of dozens of decisions, hundreds of micro-disciplines, and thousands of moments when you stayed patient instead of forcing action. Mastery feels invisible until the day it becomes obvious.

What changed everything for me was realizing that the plateau wasn't a punishment—it was proof of stability. A flat curve meant my losses were controlled, my mistakes were shrinking, and my consistency was strengthening.

The chaos had ended. The groundwork for growth had begun.

In trading, the curve of mastery always looks the same: long periods of steady effort with no external reward—followed by a sharp rise once the internal structure is strong enough. That rise is earned, not luck. And once the curve begins to bend upward, it doesn't flatten quickly. Momentum grows. Confidence grows. Clarity grows.

If you're in that flat part now, stay there. Don't abandon the path just because you haven't seen the reward yet. You're closer than you think. The plateau isn't the end of the journey—it's the phase before acceleration.

Mastery rewards the trader who endures long enough for their curve to finally rise.

The Patience Dividend

Exponential Growth Curve

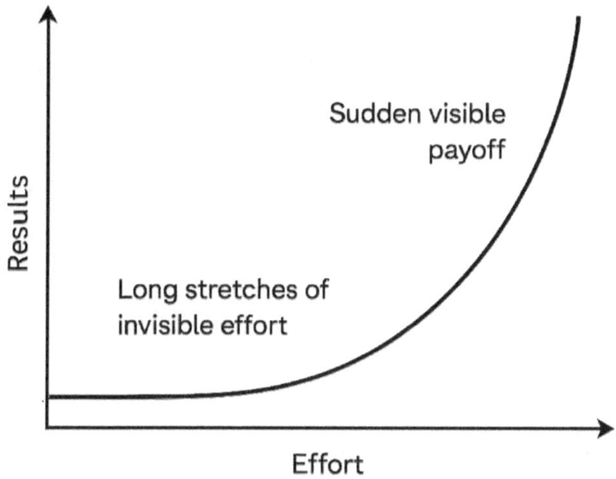

Chapter 7 - Process Over Outcome

One of the biggest shifts in my trading came the moment I stopped obsessing over results and started obsessing over the process. For years, I believed success was measured in wins and losses. But the market doesn't reward emotion or hope. It rewards consistency, structure, and execution.

The truth is simple: outcomes are unpredictable, but your process is fully in your control.

When I focused on P&L, every win felt like validation and every loss felt like failure. My emotions swung with every candle. I wasn't trading my system—I was trading my feelings about the result. That kind of pressure destroys clarity. It leads to chasing losses, forcing trades, and abandoning rules.

Process is what stabilizes you. It removes the emotional weight from every individual trade and makes the outcome almost irrelevant. When you shift your focus from "Did I win?" to "Did I execute correctly?" everything changes. You detach from randomness and anchor yourself in discipline.

The funny thing is, when you stop chasing results, the results improve. You become calmer. You trade less. You wait for alignment. You protect your capital. You execute cleanly. Over time, your equity curve stops looking like chaos and starts looking like structure.

A strong process has three pillars:

Preparation
Execution
Review

Preparation builds confidence before the trade.
Execution tests your discipline during the trade.
Review sharpens your understanding after the trade.

No single trade defines a trader. Your process does.

I learned to celebrate by following my rules—even on losing trades. A clean loss is progress. A sloppy win is poison. The market gives random rewards sometimes, and those rewards trick you into believing bad behavior is okay. That illusion is dangerous. It keeps traders stuck for years.

Once I embraced the process, I no longer feared losses. I understood they were feedback, not failure. I no longer chased wins—they came naturally through consistency. My goal stopped being profit and became precision. That shift turned trading from chaos into clarity.

You don't get paid for predicting.
You get paid for repeating.
Repeating your process with discipline is what builds every skill you need.

Focus on the process long enough, and the outcomes take care of themselves.

A reminder that the only thing you can control is your behavior—and that control is where consistency begins.

Process vs Outcome

Chapter 8 - What Success Really Means

Success used to mean hitting a certain dollar amount. Five hundred dollars a day, ten thousand a month, a funded payout—whatever the target was at the time. I believed success lived outside of me, measured in numbers and milestones. But the more I traded, the more I realized the market doesn't care about the number you want to hit. It only reflects the trader you are becoming.

Success, I eventually learned, is alignment—your actions matching your intentions. It is the quiet feeling of knowing you followed your rules without compromise. It is the peace of ending a session clean, regardless of whether the trade was a win or a loss.

Real success is internal, not external.

Most traders never reach this understanding. They chase the end result and ignore the behaviors required to reach it. They want the reward without the identity that supports it. But trading will always expose the gap between who you are and the trader you want to be.

Success is not the result of a big win.
Success is the result of thousands of disciplined decisions.

When you honor your rules, you win—even if the trade loses. When you break your rules, you lose—even when the trade wins. True success is measured by the consistency of your behavior, not the randomness of the market.

Success also has a deeper meaning: longevity. Anyone can have a lucky month. Very few can remain disciplined for years. Success is the ability to stay in the game long enough for mastery to reward you. It is the emotional balance to keep going when the results are slow, and the humility to stay grounded when the results are good.

I realized I was successful the moment I no longer needed the market to tell me I was doing well. I knew it from how I behaved. I knew it from how I handled losses. I knew it from how calmly I approached my sessions.

If you define success by outcomes, you will always feel incomplete.
If you define success by alignment, you never lose momentum.

Success is not a place you arrive at—it is a way you trade, a way you think, and eventually, a way you live.

A reminder that mastery begins the moment you stop chasing numbers and start embodying discipline.

Chapter 9 - The Psychology of Quitting

Quitting doesn't happen in a single moment. It happens slowly, silently, in the thoughts you don't say out loud. It begins with doubt, grows with fatigue, and takes root when you start believing the work isn't leading anywhere. I've felt that heaviness more times than I can count. Not because I hated trading, but because I didn't think I was progressing fast enough.

Most traders quit not because they're incapable—but because the journey feels longer than they expected.

Quitting is rarely about skill. It's about exhaustion. Emotional exhaustion from losing. Mental exhaustion from uncertainty. Spiritual exhaustion from showing up day after day without seeing the reward yet. It's the weight of being your own motivation when everything inside you feels drained.

The truth is, every trader reaches a point where quitting feels easier than continuing.
This is normal.
This is human.
This is expected.

But quitting also has a psychology of its own. It's not the absence of desire—it's the presence of pain. Pain from inconsistency. Pain from self-doubt. Pain from seeing temporary losses as a permanent verdict.

When I felt closest to quitting, it wasn't because the market beat me—it was because I misunderstood the season I was in. I thought I was failing when I was really learning. I mistook slow progress for no progress. I mistook the plateau for the end instead of the beginning.

Here's the part most people never hear: mastery has a "quiet season." A season where nothing grand happens, where results seem flat, where your growth is internal and invisible. That is where most traders quit—right before the curve rises.

Quitting never comes from lack of ability.
It comes from lack of perspective.

When I understood this, everything shifted. Instead of asking, "Why is this taking so long?" I began asking, "Who am I becoming while I wait?" That question changed how I interpreted challenges. Losses became data. Plateaus became training. Slow periods became preparation.

The temptation to quit doesn't disappear. It becomes something you recognize, understand, and move through. You stop taking it personally. You stop believing it defines you. And eventually, you stop being afraid of it.

The traders who succeed aren't the most talented—they are the ones who endure long enough to see what their discipline creates.

Quitting is a decision. Staying is a commitment. Mastery lives on the other side of that commitment.

Emotional Cycle of a Trader

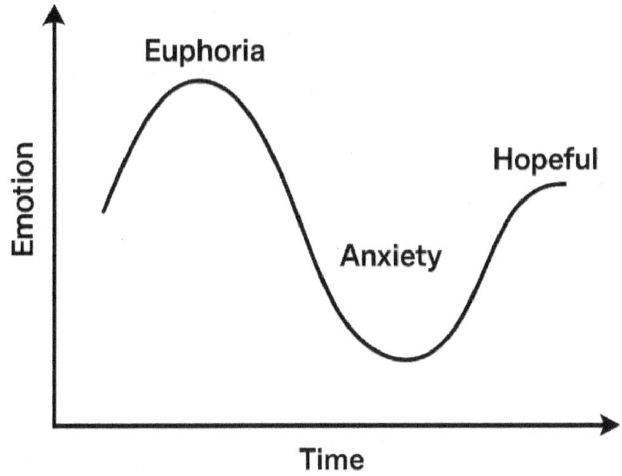

Chapter 10 - How Structure Saved My Sanity

There was a time when trading felt chaotic. I woke up at different hours, analyzed charts randomly, and took trades based on whatever emotion was strongest that day. Some days I felt confident. Other days I felt anxious. My results reflected the inconsistency of my structure. Every session felt like I was starting from scratch.

The breakthrough came when I realized that structure isn't something you add to trading—it is something trading requires to survive.

Structure became my anchor. It saved me from myself. It reduced the emotional load by eliminating endless decisions. I created fixed hours, a fixed routine, a fixed checklist, and a fixed way of reviewing trades. I didn't realize how much energy I wasted making the same decisions every day—decisions structure could have made for me.

The more structure I added, the more freedom I gained. Clear rules removed hesitation. Fixed times removed randomness. A consistent checklist removed doubt. When you reduce the number of decisions you make, your discipline increases automatically.

My structure became simple:

One trade per session.
Fixed SL and TP.
Specific entry windows.
Clear ATR thresholds.

Cancel the trade if it doesn't trigger.
Journal the outcome whether it wins or loses.

This routine became a shield. On days when my emotions were loud, the structure kept me quiet. On days when the market tempted me to overtrade, the rules held me back. Structure doesn't eliminate emotion—it prevents emotion from controlling you.

Over time, I noticed something powerful: my trading improved not because my strategy got better, but because my behavior became consistent. I wasn't reacting to the market anymore. I was following a rhythm.

Structure turns chaos into clarity.

It's not about making the perfect plan. It's about building a structure so solid that even on your worst days, you still trade like your best self. That is what saved me. That is what keeps me grounded.

Without structure, discipline fades.
With structure, discipline becomes automatic.

A reminder that your system is only as strong as the routine that protects it.

The Discipline Loop

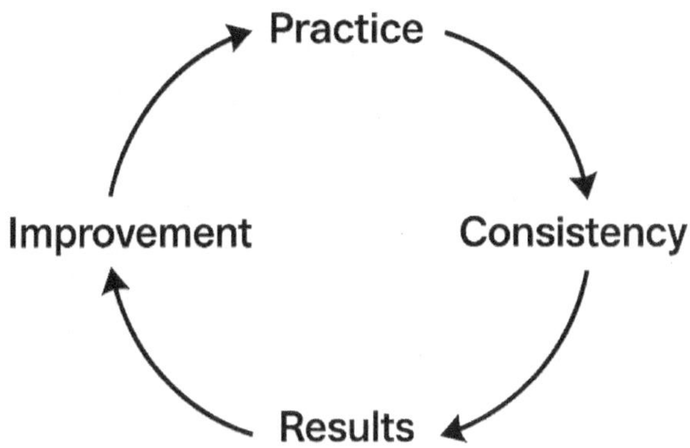

Chapter 11 - Emotional Resilience

Emotional resilience is the ability to stay centered when the market tries to pull you apart. It's not about avoiding frustration or fear—those emotions will always appear. Resilience is your capacity to feel them fully without letting them dictate your decisions.

In my early years, a single loss could destroy my entire session. One red candle felt like a personal attack. One mistake felt like the end of my progress. I didn't realize the market wasn't hurting me—my interpretation of the moment was. Every emotional reaction I had came from stories I told myself:
"I should have taken profit earlier."
"I knew I shouldn't have taken that trade."
"I have to make it back."

Those stories were louder than my rules, and that's what broke me.

Resilience began the day I stopped arguing with reality. A loss wasn't a punishment—it was data. A missed trade wasn't failure—it was information. A slow session wasn't a setback—it was part of the rhythm. When I stopped personalizing the market, I stopped collapsing emotionally.

Resilience grows in layers:

Awareness
Acceptance
Adjustment

Awareness means noticing your emotional state before it controls you.
Acceptance means allowing the feeling without resisting it.
Adjustment means returning to your process instead of reacting.

The more I practiced this, the faster I recovered. A loss that used to ruin my whole day now lasts a few minutes. A mistake that used to spiral into revenge trading now becomes a note in my journal. My emotions didn't disappear—they lost their power over me.

I learned something important: resilience is not built during winning streaks. It is built during the moments when trading feels heavy, when the market tests your conviction, when discipline feels harder than usual. Those are the moments that strengthen you. Those are the moments that shape the trader you are becoming.

Now, when I experience frustration, fear, or doubt, I don't try to suppress it. I recognize it as part of the journey. I breathe. I step away if needed. I return when my mind is clear.

Emotional resilience is not staying calm all the time—it is returning to calm faster each time you lose it.

In trading, your edge isn't just your strategy.
Your greatest edge is how quickly you regain balance.

Chapter 12 - The Patience Creed

Patience isn't just something you practice. It's something you become. Over time, I realized that patience is an identity—one you must choose every day, especially when the market gives you reasons not to. To keep myself aligned, I created a set of statements that grounded me. I called it the Patience Creed.

These lines are not rules. They are reminders—anchors that keep your mind steady when everything around you feels uncertain.

I do not rush.
Rushing is fear in motion.

I do not chase.
Chasing is the destruction of clarity.

I do not force trades.
My edge appears when it's ready, not when I want it.

I respect the market's timing, not my own.
The setup comes when structure aligns.

I protect my capital by protecting my state of mind.
A calm trader is a consistent trader.

I trust the process even when the results are slow.
Consistency grows in silence before it grows in numbers.

I accept losses without self-judgment.
A clean loss is a disciplined decision.

I release the need to control every outcome.
My job is execution, not prediction.

I am patient because patience is strength.
Patience is clarity.
Patience is mastery.

Reading this creed before each session helped me slow down and remember who I was becoming. It reminded me that trading is not about speed—it's about presence. Not about reacting—it's about responding. The market doesn't reward aggression. It rewards patience that is rooted in intention.

Over time, these statements shaped my mindset. They aligned my behavior with who I wanted to be. They quieted my impulses and strengthened my discipline. They helped me detach from the noise, the emotions, and the illusions of urgency.

The Patience Creed is not magic. It's a mirror—a way to see yourself clearly before the market tests you.

Mastery is not found in strategy alone.
It is found in the identity you choose to operate from.

Chapter 13 - Vocabulary of Mastery

The words you use shape the way you think. The way you think shapes the way you trade. Early on, I didn't realize how much language affected my mindset. I used phrases like "I hope this trade works" or "I need to make it back," and those words created anxiety, pressure, and fear. They pushed me into decisions that had nothing to do with structure.

I began paying close attention to the vocabulary I used, both out loud and in my thoughts. I replaced reactive language with intentional language. I chose words that reflected clarity, not panic. Over time, this subtle shift transformed my entire trading identity.

Here are the words and phrases that built my foundation:

"I follow my rules."
Not "I hope this works."

"I wait for alignment."
Not "I need a trade."

"This is a clean setup."
Not "This looks good enough."

"I accept this loss."
Not "I shouldn't have lost."

"I trade my plan."
Not "I think this might work."

"I protect my capital."
Not "I have to make it back."

"I am patient."
Not "I'm behind."

"I am consistent."
Not "I'm trying."

Language is a form of self-programming. Every phrase you repeat becomes a belief, and every belief shapes your actions. When your vocabulary is rooted in patience, structure, and conviction, your decisions follow the same pattern.

Trading is mental before it is mechanical. Your words influence your emotional state, and your emotional state influences your execution. Telling yourself the right things builds discipline. Telling yourself the wrong things builds confusion.

Your vocabulary becomes your identity.
Your identity becomes your behavior.
Your behavior becomes your results.

Speak like the trader you want to become.
Act like the trader you plan to be.
Trade like the trader you're already becoming.

Chapter 14 - Closing Reflection – Staying in the Game

The longer I trade, the more I realize that the real goal is not perfection or even constant profitability. The real goal is staying in the game long enough for everything you've learned to turn into instinct. Most traders don't fail because they're incapable—they fail because they leave the game before their discipline matures.

Staying in the game requires humility. You must accept that some days you will lose, some weeks will feel slow, and some months will test everything you believe about yourself. But that doesn't mean you're failing. It means you're evolving. Growth is not loud. It doesn't announce itself. It unfolds quietly, session by session, rule by rule.

There were times when I thought I had reached my limit. Times when the setbacks felt heavier than the progress. Times when I questioned whether I belonged in this world at all. But every time I paused instead of quitting, I discovered something new in myself—strength I didn't know I had, discipline I didn't know I could build, and patience I didn't know I could sustain.

What kept me going was simple: I decided that trading wasn't something I did. It was part of who I was becoming. I wasn't chasing a payout. I was building a mindset. And once I embraced that identity, everything changed. Trading became clearer. Simpler. Lighter.

If there is one truth I want you to carry forward, it is this:

The traders who succeed are not the ones who never struggle.
They are the ones who choose to continue—steadily, humbly, patiently.

Staying in the game is the real victory.
Because if you stay long enough, mastery always reveals itself.

This is the end of Phase One.
Now that the foundation is built, we move into the structure, rules, and tools that bring everything together.

Phase Two - Strategy and Execution

The work you've done in Phase One builds the mindset required for consistency. Now we move into the mechanical side of trading—the structure, setups, rules, and behaviors that translate mindset into measurable execution.

Phase Two is not about complexity.
It is about clarity, repetition, and precision.

Your discipline from Phase One becomes the engine.
These chapters become the steering wheel.

Section 1

The Foundation of Price

Before indicators, before prop-firms, before strategy, there is price.
Understanding price is understanding the language of the market. Every candle, every swing, every level tells a story about who is in control, who is trapped, and where imbalance is building.

This section teaches you how to read that story with clarity.

We begin with the building blocks of price action: candlesticks, structure, and key levels.

Chapter 15 - The Language of Candlesticks

Candlesticks are the market's handwriting. Every wick, body, and close reveals who is winning the battle between buyers and sellers. Before you understand any strategy, you must learn to read this language. It's the foundation of every decision you'll make as a trader.

A candle is more than a shape—it's a story of intention, aggression, hesitation, imbalance, and resolution. When you learn to read that story, you stop guessing and start interpreting.

A strong bullish candle tells you buyers were confident enough to close price near the high.
A long wick shows rejection—an area where one side pushed but couldn't maintain control.
A small body shows indecision—neither side willing to commit.

This is not about memorizing candle patterns. It's about understanding the psychology behind them. A candle is not a signal. It is information.

The open shows where the battle began.
The close shows who won that battle.
The wicks show where the losing side tried—and failed—to push the market.

Once you begin to see candles as a reflection of human emotions, they become clearer. You can spot aggression versus hesitation. Strength versus weakness. Continuation versus exhaustion.

Price leaves clues, and those clues repeat every day.

The most important lesson I learned is this: a single candle means nothing without context. A bullish candle in the middle of nowhere is noise. A bullish candle breaking out of structure with rising volume is momentum. The candle itself isn't the signal. The environment is.

This chapter lays the groundwork for every setup that follows. When you truly understand the language of candlesticks, you no longer need to force trades. The chart begins speaking to you in a way that feels natural and predictable.

Candles don't lie. They reveal.

Chapter 16 - Structure Before Strategy

Before you can trade any setup with confidence, you must understand structure—the framework that gives the market shape. Structure shows you where price is moving, why it is moving, and where traders are likely to make decisions. Without it, every candle feels random. With it, the chart begins to make sense.

Structure is built from three core elements:

Swing highs
Swing lows
Liquidity

Swing highs mark where buyers stopped pushing.
Swing lows mark where sellers lost pressure.
Liquidity marks where trapped traders wait to be freed.

The market moves from one pool of liquidity to another. It isn't random—it's purposeful. Large players need liquidity to fill orders, and price naturally gravitates toward areas where traders have placed stops, entries, or pending orders. Understanding this makes the market feel less chaotic and more intentional.

When you identify structure correctly, you can see the rhythm of the market. You notice how price expands, pulls back, and expands again. You see the buildup before the breakout. You recognize when a trend is weakening or when a reversal is setting up.

Structure reveals the path.
Strategy simply tells you when to walk it.

Many traders skip this step. They jump straight into indicators or signals without understanding the map those signals operate on. That's why they get confused, frustrated, and inconsistent. They're trying to navigate without knowing the terrain.

Learning structure changed everything for me. It helped me stop forcing trades. It showed me where price was "inviting" a move and where it was exhausted. It helped me avoid taking entries in the middle of nowhere and taught me to wait until price reached logical zones with real strength behind them.

When you master structure, you master context.
And when you master context, your strategy starts working the way it was designed to.

Structure is not optional—it is the backbone of precision.

Chapter 17 - Support, Resistance and Context

Support and resistance are more than lines on a chart. They are memories—areas where traders made decisions, felt emotions, experienced regret, or found confidence. The market remembers these areas because traders remember them. Every retest carries the emotional weight of what happened there before.

Support is where buyers previously proved they were willing to defend price.
Resistance is where sellers previously showed they were willing to apply pressure.

Most traders draw these levels mechanically. But the real power comes from understanding *why* price reacted there in the first place. Was there trapped liquidity? A strong rejection wick? A consolidation base? A breakout level? The more context you attach to a level, the more meaningful it becomes.

A level without context is just a guess.
A level with context becomes a signal.

What matters most is not the line itself—it's what the market did *before* and *after* touching it. Did price explode away from it? Did it hesitate and coil? Did wicks aggressively reject it? Did volume confirm the reaction?

Context transforms a simple line into a story:

A failed breakout becomes a trap.
A retest becomes confirmation.

A consolidation becomes a launch point.
A rejection becomes imbalance.

When I learned to view support and resistance through the lens of context, my trading changed. I stopped reacting to every touch and started waiting for the narrative to form. The market was no longer random—it was logical, layered, and intentional.

Here is the simple truth:

Support and resistance are not signals.
They are locations—locations where signals might appear.

Once you combine these levels with structure, volume, and volatility, you get clarity. You understand when a level is strong or weak, when it is likely to break, and when it is likely to reverse.

Support and resistance do not predict the future—they reveal the battlefield.

Context gives you the confidence to wait for the right moment.
Patience gives you the discipline to act only when alignment appears.

Support and resistance matter, but context makes them powerful.

Support & Resistance

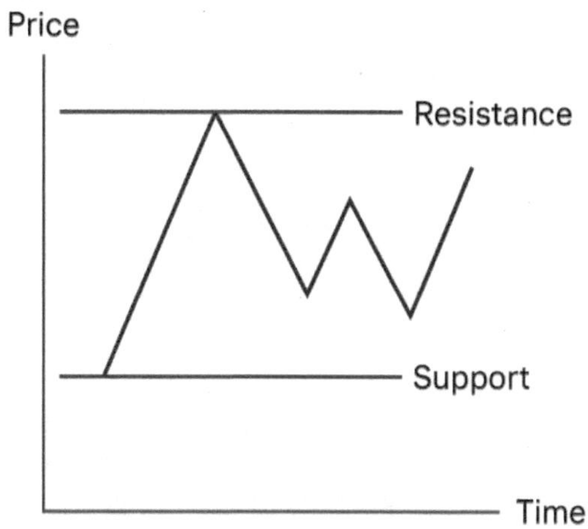

Section 2
Tools of Precision

Once you understand price, structure, and context, tools become amplifiers—not crutches. Indicators don't predict the market; they interpret it. When used correctly, they provide clarity, confidence, and confirmation. When misused, they create confusion and dependency.

This section focuses on the tools that support your decision-making without replacing your judgment: VWAP, DEMA, ATR, and Volume.

These tools help filter noise, measure volatility, and confirm momentum so your execution becomes cleaner and more consistent.

Chapter 18 - Indicators That Serve, Not Lead

Most traders begin their journey by searching for the perfect indicator—some magical tool that will predict direction, eliminate uncertainty, and protect them from losses. I know because I did the same. My charts once looked like a Christmas tree—RSI, MACD, Bollinger Bands, Stochastic, Ichimoku, multiple EMAs. The more clutter I added, the less clarity I had.

Eventually, I learned a truth that changed everything:

The cleaner the chart, the clearer the mind.

Indicators were never meant to lead.
They were created to *assist*—to refine what price and structure already revealed.

Every indicator you see on a chart is simply a delayed reflection of price.
Price moves first; indicators follow.
So giving indicators more authority than raw price is like trusting an echo more than the original sound.

Once this clicked, I stripped everything down to four essentials:

VWAP — The Session's Anchor

VWAP shows where most of the money is positioned.
Above it: buyers dominate.
Below it: sellers dominate.
Far from it: the market is emotional and stretched.
Close to it: balance, hesitation, or manipulation.

VWAP tells you *where crowd memory lives.*

DEMA (9/20) — Momentum Without Noise

The 9/20 DEMA cross isn't a signal to trade—it's a clue.
It shows whether short-term pressure is increasing or fading.
It helps frame rhythm, not predict direction.

Use DEMA to confirm what structure already suggests.

ATR — The Volatility Speedometer

ATR is not optional.
It defines every bracket you place—your stop-loss, your take-profit, your risk.

ATR = How much room the market needs to breathe.
If you ignore ATR, you suffocate your trade.
If you respect it, your bracket matches the market's rhythm—not your hope.

Volume — The Voice of Conviction

Price is the body.
Volume is the heartbeat.

A breakout without volume is a whisper.
A breakout with volume is a declaration.

Volume tells you if participation is real or if price is pretending.

The Principle That Changed My Trading Forever:

Price leads. Structure explains. Indicators confirm.
Never the reverse.

When indicators serve instead of lead, clarity replaces confusion.
Your screen becomes quieter.
Your decisions become cleaner.
Your emotions stabilize.
Your confidence grows.

Because mastery isn't about having more tools—
it's about needing less.

Chapter 19 - Understanding ATR & Volatility Windows

ATR changed my trading more than any indicator, rule, or mindset shift.
Not because it predicts direction—it doesn't—but because it tells the truth most traders ignore:

You can't trade every market condition the same.

Price has a rhythm.
Volatility has cycles.
Momentum has seasons.
ATR reveals all three.

Most traders trade without knowing how far the market can realistically move.
They set stops too tight, targets too wide, or trade during dead volatility windows expecting movement that simply isn't there.

ATR fixed all of that.

What ATR Actually Measures

ATR shows how much the market typically moves per candle.
That one number controls:

- Your stop-loss

- Your take-profit
- Whether the session is valid
- Whether the breakout has room
- Whether the trade is even worth taking

Without ATR, your bracket is guesswork.
With ATR, your bracket is precision.

Volatility Windows — The Market's Breathing Cycle

Every market has windows where volatility expands and contracts.
Ignoring these windows is like trying to surf without knowing when waves form.

Here are the three major windows:

7 PM ET — Globex Open (Calm → Slow Pressure)

- ATR starts small
- Volume is thin
- Moves are cleaner but quieter

- Ideal for mechanical stop orders
- Brackets must be tighter

This window teaches discipline—not excitement.

---

2 AM ET — London Open (Surge → Continuation)

- ATR expands
- Breakouts follow-through more cleanly
- Volume confirms early
- Structure respects itself
- Best session for technical traders

London is where "quiet patience" turns into "clean precision."

8:30–10:30 AM ET — New York (Chaos → Momentum)

- ATR peaks

- Liquidity explodes
- News whipsaws test emotional stability
- Best window for strong breakouts *if* volume confirms
- After 10:30 AM: volatility dies and chop takes over

New York rewards discipline but punishes impatience.

How ATR Controls Your Bracket

Your bracket adapts to ATR.
Your rules do not.

For example (Gold):

ATR	Stop (pts)	Target (pts)	R:R
8–9	18	36	1:2
10–12	24	48	1:2
13–15	30	60	1:2

For YM:

ATR	Stop (pts)	Target (pts)
25	50	100
30	60	120

If ATR is below threshold: skip
Not because you're scared—because the math says so.

The Golden Rule:

Trade conditions, not opinions.

ATR tells you whether the market has room to support your setup.
If ATR is dead, you cannot force volatility into existence.
If ATR is alive, follow your rules and let the structure work.

When you sync your bracket to volatility, your entire trading life changes:

- Stops stop getting randomly hit
- Targets actually get reached
- Breakouts follow through cleanly
- Your trust in the system grows

- Your consistency stabilizes

ATR isn't just a tool.
It's the boundary between professional calm and emotional chaos.

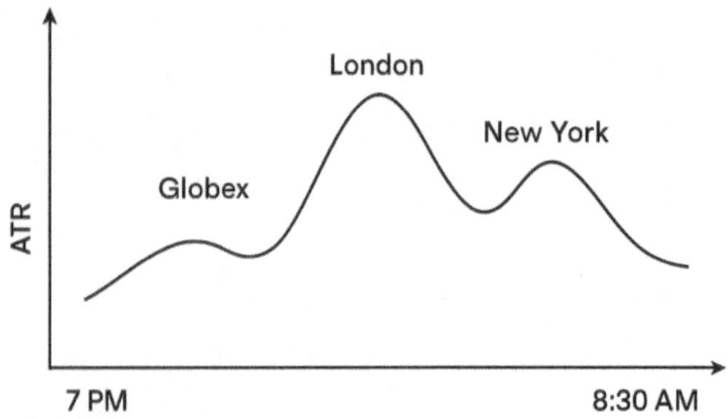

Volatility breathes – adapt your bracket to its rhythm.

Chapter 20 — Risk-to-Reward: The Mathematics of Confidence

Most traders obsess over entries. They search for signals, indicators, patterns, and timing, believing that consistency comes from predicting direction accurately. But direction is only half of the equation. The real engine of long-term consistency is risk-to-reward—the silent ratio controlling whether your system wins over time.

Risk-to-reward is more than math; it's psychology. It shapes your behavior, your discipline, and your ability to stay stable during drawdowns. Before I understood R:R, I chased precision. After I understood it, I chased alignment. The difference is everything.

Why Risk-to-Reward Matters More Than Win Rate

Most traders try to "be right," not profitable. That mindset keeps you trapped. A trader with a 40% win rate using a 1:2 R:R can outperform a trader winning 70% of the time with a 1:1 ratio.

Here's the truth no one likes to accept:

Win rate makes you feel good.
Risk-to-reward makes you succeed.

At 1:1, a single emotional loss can erase five wins. At 1:2, the math protects your psychology. You don't need to win often—you need to win *properly*.

The 1:2 Ratio — Your Psychological Edge

My entire system lives on one rule:

Risk 1 to make 2. Every time. No exceptions.

Why?

- A clean 1:2 ratio forces discipline.
- It prevents shrinking stops out of fear.
- It kills the urge to take profit early.
- It makes losing less emotional, because two wins erase four losses.
- It removes the need to chase high win rates.

1:2 turns trading into a game of *execution*, not prediction. That shift saved my career.

Expectancy — The Formula Professionals Live By

Every system has a mathematical heartbeat called expectancy:

Expectancy = (Win Rate × Average Win) – (Loss Rate × Average Loss)

A 40% win rate with a 1:2 R:R produces positive expectancy.

A 70% win rate with a 1:1 R:R often produces negative expectancy.

Your goal isn't to win every day—
your goal is to maintain positive expectancy over time.

Why Breaking R:R Breaks Everything

Every time you:

- move your stop to avoid losing,
- shrink your stop because you're scared,
- grab profit early because you fear reversal,

—you break the math your system depends on.

A broken ratio destroys confidence.
A broken ratio kills discipline.
A broken ratio forces revenge trades.

You cannot build mastery on emotional math.

The Three R:R Traps That Destroy Traders

1. Moving Stops to "Give It More Room"

This is fear pretending to be patience.
When you increase risk but don't increase reward, you flip the ratio in the market's favor.

2. Taking Profit Early

Greed doesn't always look like chasing trades.
Sometimes it looks like *closing too soon*.

A trader who consistently cuts winners destroys the only advantage a 1:2 ratio gives.

3. Chasing Home Runs

Aiming for 1:5 or 1:8 sounds impressive, but it creates hesitation, overthinking, and impatience.
The system becomes inconsistent because the trader becomes inconsistent.

Small, steady wins with a fixed 1:2 ratio build a career—not lottery-style trades.

Examples: How R:R Protects You Emotionally

Two traders take the same five trades.

Trader A (1:1 R:R)
Wins 3 → +3R
Loses 2 → −2R
Outcome: +1R

But one emotional mistake drops the entire week to negative.

Trader B (1:2 R:R)
Wins 2 → +4R
Loses 3 → −3R
Outcome: +1R

Lower win rate. Same results. Bigger stability.

And if Trader B wins a third trade?

Outcome: +3R
Massively profitable.

This is how professionals survive losing streaks and scale accounts calmly—through math, not emotion.

R:R and the ORB Setup

Your Opening Range Breakout follows the perfect formula:

- 1 trade per session
- stop-loss based on ATR
- take-profit based on 2× ATR
- hands-off execution

This system works *because* the R:R is fixed.
It's the backbone of your consistency.

Confidence Comes From Math, Not Emotion

You don't need certainty to enter a trade.
You need structure and a ratio that keeps you alive when uncertainty strikes.

At 1:2:

- Your losses become manageable.
- Your wins create cushion.
- Your mind stays calm.
- Your discipline becomes instinct.

The market doesn't reward the trader who is right the most—it rewards the trader who protects his ratio.

The R:R Promise

If you honor 1:2 every session—
If you protect your stop-loss—
If you let your winners reach target—
If you treat the ratio as non-negotiable—

Consistency becomes inevitable.

A trader who protects R:R protects his future.

End-of-Chapter Reflection

Risk-to-reward is not a setting.
It is the belief that long-term success depends more on behavior than prediction.
Protect the ratio, and the ratio will protect you.

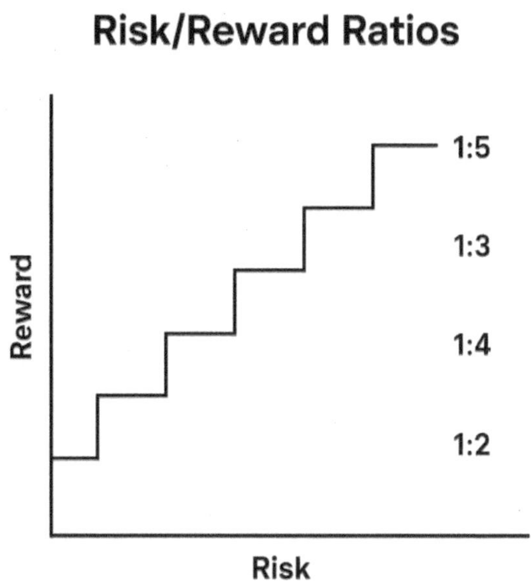

Chapter 21 - Volume & Momentum Confirmation

Volume is the *truth serum* of the market.
Price can lie.
Wicks can deceive.
Breakouts can fake.
But volume never lies — because it reveals who is actually participating.

You cannot have real momentum without real participation.
You cannot have a real breakout without real conviction.
This is why volume is one of the most important filters in your ORB system.

Price = Result. Volume = Effort.

If price moves far with low volume, the move is weak.
If price barely moves with high volume, pressure is building.
When both expand together—range + volume—momentum is real.

This is the "secret" behind clean, powerful breakouts.

The Volume Baseline (Your North Star)

Every instrument has a normal rhythm.

Before placing any ORB trade, compare the breakout candle's volume to the baseline:

Baseline = average of the last 3–5 candles

You want the breakout candle to have:

≥ 1.2× the baseline

This is your confirmation that real traders—not just the algorithmic noise—are behind the move.

Without this filter:

- You enter weak breakouts
- You get trapped in fake pushes
- You constantly get wicked out
- You blame your system when it was simply no volume

Volume is your shield.

Accumulation → Expansion → Momentum

Volume tells you when the market is preparing to move.

Accumulation (Quiet Volume)

- Tight candles
- Small bodies
- Wicks shrinking
- VWAP acting as a magnet
- ATR low but rising
  This is the inhale.

Expansion (Volume spike + wide candle)

This is the moment your stop order triggers.
This is the exhale.

Momentum (Continuation candles)

Clear direction, clean follow-through, no hesitation.

When you understand these three phases, ORB stops being luck and becomes timing.

Effort vs. Result

One of the most powerful concepts in momentum trading:

When effort increases and result increases → strong trend

(volume up + range up)

When effort increases but result stalls → exhaustion

(volume up + range flat)

When effort decreases but result increases → trap

(volume down + range up)

This is how professionals avoid getting caught in fakeouts.

Volume Spikes — Friend or Warning?

Not all volume spikes mean continuation. Some mean exhaustion.

Continuation Spike:

- Appears early in the breakout
- Solid body candle
- Clean ORB range break
- ATR aligning

Exhaustion Spike:

- Appears after a long run
- Huge wick
- Candle closes weak
- Followed by hesitation

Continuation means "join the move." Exhaustion means "exit the move."

Knowing the difference removes 80% of fake entries.

Why ORB + Volume Is So Elite

A clean ORB with a confirmed volume spike is one of the most reliable momentum structures in the world.

Because it combines:

- Structure (the range)
- Volatility (ATR threshold)
- Momentum (volume)
- Execution discipline (stop orders, 1 trade per session)

This is why your system works WHEN you apply all 3 filters:

1. Clean ORB
2. ATR above threshold
3. Volume ≥ 1.2× baseline

Miss one?
Skip the trade.
Never force alignment.

Volume is the voice. Price is the echo. Listen to the voice.

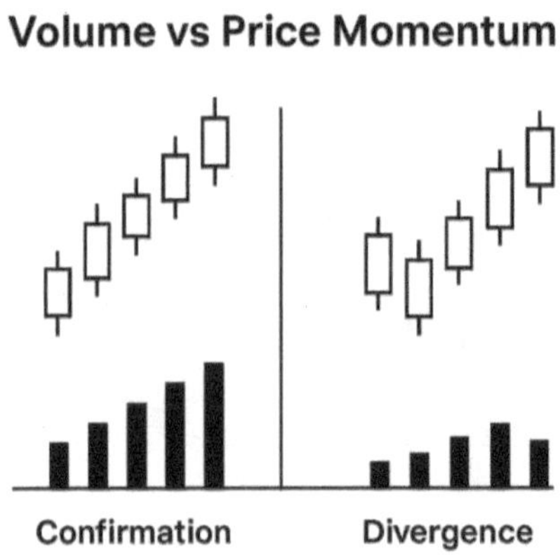

Effort (volume) must match result (price).

Chapter 22 - The 15-Minute Opening Range Breakout (ORB)

(Your Signature Setup — Mechanical, Simple, Repeatable)

Every trader needs one setup they can trust with their life.
Not ten. Not five. One.

The ORB is that setup.

It is clean. It is visual. It removes emotion.
And it reveals the session's intention better than anything else on your chart.

The beauty of the ORB is that the market tells you exactly what it wants to do — you simply wait for confirmation.

Why the ORB Works

Because the *first 15 minutes* of every session reflect pure emotion:

- Fear (overnight positions unwinding)
- Excitement (news and anticipation)
- Institutional orders being released
- Retail reacting to the first pulse of movement

The candlestick formed during this window becomes the session's truth.

Marking its high and low creates the Opening Range — the "battlefield" from which the rest of the session will unfold.

Break above? Buyers win.
Break below? Sellers win.
Stay inside? No trade.

Simple. Elegant. Powerful.

Your Three ORB Sessions

You trade three specific windows because each carries a unique behavioral signature:

7:00 PM ET — Globex (Calm, Mechanical)

- Low volume
- Clean structure
- Perfect for mechanical stop orders
- Little emotion → ideal for data-driven execution

2:00 AM ET — London (Technical Trend Window)

- Strong liquidity
- Clear directional bias
- High probability continuation
- Great for disciplined structure traders

8:30–10:30 AM ET — New York (High Emotion, High Volume)

- News reactions
- Breaks with force
- Can produce the largest moves
- Requires volume confirmation and ATR compliance

Each session is a mirror.
Globex tests patience.
London tests structure.
New York tests emotional discipline.

The Mechanics of the ORB (Your Exact Process)

1. Mark the first 15-minute candle

- Globex: 7:00–7:15 PM
- London: 2:00–2:15 AM
- New York: 8:30–8:45 AM

2. Draw the Range

- High = Buy Stop trigger
- Low = Sell Stop trigger

3. Apply Filters (non-negotiable)

You only trade if all three confirm:

✓ ATR meets threshold

(Gold ≥ 9, YM ≥ 25)

✓ Volume ≥ 1.2× baseline on the breakout candle

✓ ORB structure is clean

(no overlapping consolidation or erratic wicks)

4. Place Stop Orders

- Buy Stop: a few ticks above the ORB high
- Sell Stop: a few ticks below the ORB low
  Hands off. No interference.

5. Let the Market Trigger You In

If it breaks with volume → you're in.
If it never breaks → you're out (no trade).
If it forms fake wicks → skip.

6. One Trade Per Session

No second chances.
No re-entries.
No "maybe this one works."

7. Session Cutoff Rule (Your Lifeline)

After:

- 10:30 AM ET (NY)
- 3:00 AM ET (London)
- 8:00 PM ET (Globex)

Cancel all unfilled orders.
Discipline before opportunity.

Why This Setup Changes Lives

Because it teaches:

- Patience (waiting for the range)

- Discipline (only one trade)
- Structure (mechanical entries)
- Risk management (fixed bracket)
- Self-control (no touching the trade)
- Consistency (daily repeatable routine)

Most traders lose because they trade too much.
You win by trading only one clean moment.

The ORB forces you to respect timing, structure, and psychology.

It is the perfect setup for a funded account and for multi-account scaling.

The Opening Range Reveals Everything — If you are patient enough to listen.

Chapter 23 - Gold, Indices, and Session Behavior

(Understanding the Personality of Each Market You Trade)

Every market has a personality.
Every session has a rhythm.
And every trader has a temperament.

Your consistency was built the moment you matched your temperament to the right market during the right session — instead of fighting against who you are.

You don't trade *charts*.
You trade behavior, timing, and emotion — yours and the market's.

This chapter teaches you to understand the "dialects" of price action so you never misread the environment again.

GOLD (GC / MGC / XAUUSD)

The Emotional Instrument

Gold is pure emotion.
Fear, liquidity shifts, sentiment — Gold reacts to all of it.

Gold is the fastest and most sensitive instrument you trade.
It rewards precision and punishes impatience.

How Gold Behaves

- During low volume: it drifts, fakes out, and chops.
- During volatility windows (2AM / 8:30AM): it explodes.
- During news: it overreacts fast and often reverses.

Gold teaches discipline because it exposes every flaw instantly.

Your Gold Rules

- ATR must be ≥ 9 → otherwise skip.
- VWAP distance must be clean (≥ 8 pts).
- Volume must confirm breakout (≥ 1.2× baseline).
- 1 trade per session ONLY.

Gold is your mirror — if you're emotional, it will show you.

YM (Dow Futures)

The Structured Giant

YM is slow, heavy, and deliberate.
Compared to Gold, it feels like steering a ship instead of a motorcycle.

It respects structure beautifully:

- Clean HH/HL sequences
- Consistent retests
- Gradual shifts in trend

YM hates chaos. It loves rhythm.

Personality Traits

- Mornings move best (9–10:30 AM ET)
- Tends to trap early then reveal true bias
- Breakouts need volume confirmation
- Best used for calm mechanical trading

Where Gold is emotional, YM is logical.

ES (S&P Futures)

The Market's Heartbeat

ES is the most balanced instrument on your screen.
Not too fast, not too slow — the perfect "middle child."

This is why you use ES as:

- A thermometer
- A bias confirmer
- A sentiment gauge

If Gold and YM disagree, you look at ES.
It speaks the "truth" more often than either of them.

ES Behavior

- Smooth structure
- Clean ORB reactions
- Deep volume participation
- Ideal for trend confirmation

You don't need to trade ES to benefit from it.
Every funded trader should use ES as a *context instrument.*

SESSION PERSONALITIES

(The Secret That Most Traders Never Learn)

Each session isn't just a time on the clock — it's a psychological environment.

7:00 PM ET — Globex

Personality: Calm, mechanical, emotionless
Best for: Simple stop-order ORB execution
Your advantage: No noise → clean structure
Caution: Don't manually click entries. Let the stops do the work.

Globex rewards patience.

2:00 AM ET — London

Personality: Technical, structured, directional
Best for: Traders who love clean ORBs and true volatility
Rhythm:

- 2:00–2:30 AM → initial burst
- 2:30–3:00 AM → continuation or reversal
- 3:00–3:30 AM → the real trend appears

London rewards skill and discipline.

8:30–10:30 AM ET — New York

Personality: Emotional, explosive, crowded
Best for: Experienced breakout traders
Requirements:

- Volume confirmation
- ATR compliance
- Zero emotion

Rule: No trades after 10:30 AM — edge dies here.

New York rewards emotional control.

THE FINAL TRUTH

Choosing an instrument is choosing a lifestyle.
Choosing a session is choosing a mindset.
Choosing a breakout is choosing a version of yourself.

When your temperament matches the personality of the market,
trading stops feeling like chaos... and starts feeling like alignment.

Chapter 24 - Managing One Trade Per Session

(The Rule That Saved My Account — and My Mind)

There will come a moment in every trader's journey where they realize this truth:

You don't need more trades.
You need fewer mistakes.

The instant I committed to one trade per session, everything about my trading transformed:

- My anxiety dropped
- My execution sharpened
- My results stabilized
- My confidence grew
- My discipline matured

Not because the strategy changed —
but because I finally eliminated the chaos.

WHY ONE TRADE WORKS

Most traders don't fail because of technique; they fail because of overexposure.

Overtrading does 4 silent things that destroy consistency:

1. Dilutes your edge
2. Increases emotional volatility
3. Triggers revenge behavior
4. Makes outcomes random instead of structured

One trade per session forces your brain to:

- prepare
- wait
- respect rules
- treat every decision with weight

When you only have one bullet, you aim with care.

THE ONE-TRADE FRAMEWORK

Below is the exact structure that rebuilt your discipline and consistency.

---

1. Pre-Market Preparation (10–15 minutes before session)

- Check ATR
- Check VWAP distance
- Check structure (4H → 1H → 15M)
- Mark 15-minute ORB
- Confirm volume behavior
- Ensure session personality aligns
- Confirm rule alignment (no fatigue, no emotion)

Mindset phrase:

"Today I execute, not chase."

---

2. The Execution Window

Rules:

- Stop orders only
- Hands off once bracket is placed

- No manual market entries
- No doubling size
- No second chance orders

If the breakout is clean and confirmed → you're in.
If not → you skip.

Mindset phrase:

"If it's meant to trigger, it will."

---

3. Post-Trade Review (immediately after closing)

Whether TP or SL hits:

1. Screenshot the chart
2. Log ATR
3. Log emotion
4. Log result
5. Write one line:
   "What did this session teach me?"

This repeats daily, so your improvement compounds.

Mindset phrase:

"The lesson always matters more than the result."

WHY THIS RULE FEELS LIKE MAGIC

Because it removes everything that was hurting you:

❌ Impulse trades
❌ Revenge trades
❌ Overanalyzing setups
❌ Emotional spirals
❌ Multiple losses stacking
❌ Trying to "make the day back"
❌ Hesitation from uncertainty

And it strengthens everything that makes you consistent:

✓ Patience
✓ Focus
✓ Execution quality
✓ Emotional distance
✓ Clarity
✓ Calm
✓ Habit formation

This is not a limitation.
This is liberation.

Your results improved BECAUSE
you eliminated chaos and became mechanical.

THE PROFESSIONAL MINDSET

The pros don't trade more; they trade better.

The one-trade-per-session rule is how professionals train consistency:

- No noise
- No confusion
- No emotional decision-making
- No "maybe I should try one more..."

You transform trading from a dopamine machine into a performance routine.

One shot. One bracket. One outcome. One lesson.

That's mastery.

THE FINAL TRUTH

You don't become consistent by winning more.
You become consistent by removing behaviors that destroy consistency.

The fastest path to funded stability wasn't taking more trades —
it was learning to do less, flawlessly.

Mastery rewards restraint.

Chapter 25 - The Prop-Firm Ecosystem

(Where Discipline Becomes Your Real Edge)

Prop firms changed everything for me—not because they gave me capital,
but because they forced me to grow up as a trader.

They turned trading from a hobby filled with emotions into a business built on rules, structure, and accountability.

A prop firm is not just a place to get funded;
it's a psychological testing ground.

They don't care if you can win.
They care if you can follow rules while winning.

And that is what makes prop-firm trading the most honest path to mastery.

WHAT PROP FIRMS ACTUALLY TEST

Most people think prop firms are testing these:

- Strategy
- Skill
- Chart reading

- Accuracy

But the truth is, they are testing:

- Patience
- Consistency
- Emotional control
- Risk management
- Respect for structure

Thousands of traders can win. Very few can do it inside constraints.

Prop firms are designed to reveal the truth:

Can you behave like a professional when the pressure is highest?

THE FOUR HIDDEN TESTS

Every prop firm—Topstep, Apex, Leeloo, Bulenox—tests you through the same four categories, even if they call them different names.

1. The Drawdown Test

Not: *Can you make money?*
But: *Can you protect money?*

If you cannot protect capital under constraints, you're not ready to scale.

---

2. The Boredom Test

Can you follow the plan when the market is slow and your ego is loud?

Most traders fail here — they chase action because patience feels like nothingness.
Prop-firm pros embrace boredom as proof of discipline.

---

3. The Pressure Test

Every prop account amplifies emotion:

- You're being evaluated
- There are firm rules
- One mistake can end the account
- The clock is ticking

If you don't have structure, fear or adrenaline will take the wheel.

The evaluation is not about the setup—it's about your state of mind.

---

4. The Consistency Test

Prop firms study patterns:

- Are you calm day-to-day?
- Do you size consistently?
- Do you avoid random trades?
- Do you treat losses with logic or with revenge?

If you behave erratically, they know you can't manage scalable capital.

Consistency always beats aggression.

THE SHIFT FROM "PASSING" TO "PERFORMING"

I used to treat challenges like a race:

"Let me hit target fast.
Let me pass quickly.
Let me prove I'm ready."

That mindset cost me resets, frustration, and confidence.

Over time, I learned the truth:

You don't pass a prop firm by going fast.
You pass by trading slow, calm, and mechanical.

Passing is not the goal.
Becoming the person who passes easily is.

Once that shift happens, challenges become effortless.

HOW THE PROP-FIRM WORLD ACTUALLY WORKS

Prop firms don't pay you for winning. **They pay you for consistency.**

They're not looking for gamblers who get lucky.
They're looking for traders who can:

- Survive bad days
- Control risk
- Respect structure
- Trade small but precise
- Repeat the same behavior daily

A good prop trader is boring.
Their trading is mechanical, predictable, calm.

If your trading looks exciting,
your future payouts will not be.

WHY PROP FIRMS ARE THE GREATEST TEACHER

They forge you into someone who:

- trusts structure
- trades inside boundaries
- stops when rules say stop
- trades with clarity instead of emotion
- respects daily loss limits
- protects the cushion
- operates like a professional

Prop firms expose your bad habits
and reward your good ones
faster than live trading ever will.

This ecosystem changes you—and prepares you for scaling multiple accounts, which is where the real life-changing income begins.

Prop firms are not obstacles.
They're mirrors.
They reflect the trader you actually are.

Chapter 26 - The Topstep Framework

(Where Discipline Meets Structure and Structure Builds Freedom)

Topstep wasn't just a funding company for me—it became a discipline factory, a place that broke my bad habits and rebuilt me into a trader with structure, patience, and real consistency.

This is the chapter that changed my entire trading identity.

Because Topstep doesn't simply evaluate you—they train you through pressure and rules until your behavior matches the identity of a professional.

THE TRUTH ABOUT TOPSTEP

Most traders misunderstand what Topstep actually is.

They think it's:

- A quick funding shortcut
- A way to trade bigger
- A chance to get lucky with someone else's money

But Topstep is none of these.

Topstep is a behavioral filter.

It separates:

- disciplined from undisciplined
- mechanical from emotional
- patient from impulsive
- professionals from hopefuls

And it does this through structure.

THE TOPSTEP RULES ARE NOT LIMITS — THEY ARE PROTECTION

Most traders see the rules as restrictive:

- "Daily loss limit is too tight"
- "Trailing drawdown is unfair"
- "Cutoff times kill opportunities"

But the rules are the reason professionals succeed. They force you into behaviors you should have had from the beginning:

- taking fewer trades
- respecting time windows
- protecting risk
- avoiding emotional spirals
- trading small but precise
- finishing early instead of chasing

The rules eliminate freedom so you can gain control.

Once you accept this, trading becomes calm.

MY TOPSTEP SYSTEM (THE ONE THAT FINALLY MADE ME CONSISTENT)

After years of frustration, resets, and emotional trading, I built the system that finally worked.

I share it here exactly as I use it.

✓ Account Type:

$50K Combine → Funded → Master Account

✓ Sessions I trade:

- 7 PM (Globex)
- 2 AM (London)
- 8:30–10:30 AM (New York ONLY window)

✓ One-Trade Rule:

ONE trade per session.
Not two. Not "one more try."
One. Done.

✓ ATR Filter:

- Gold ATR(15m) must be ≥ 9
- YM ATR(15m) must be ≥ 25

If below? Skip the session.

✓ Volume Filter:

ORB candle must have 1.2× baseline volume
Otherwise, skip.

✓ Clean Structure Only:

No overlapping consolidation.
No double wicks.
ORB must be clean.

✓ No Trades Past Cutoff:

- Nothing past 10:30 AM
- All positions closed by 10:30 AM

✓ Risk:

1:2 R:R
Bracket set in advance
Never adjusted manually
Never widened

✓ Weekly Risk Cap:

$300 per account
If hit → STOP trading for the week

✓ Monthly Risk Cap:

$600 per account
If hit → STOP trading for the month

This system is not glamorous.
It's boring.
Mechanical.
Predictable.

That's why it works.

THE CUSHION MINDSET

This was the breakthrough that changed everything.

Your goal in Topstep is NOT to make money. Your goal is to build a cushion.

The cushion is your oxygen tank. Your grounding. Your breathing room.

Once I stopped trying to "hit big numbers" and instead focused on:

- protecting the cushion
- expanding the cushion
- trading conservatively
- letting compounding handle the rest

My entire trading identity shifted from emotional to mechanical.

The cushion is what makes you calm.

Calm is what makes you consistent.

Consistency is what keeps you funded.

Topstep didn't change my strategy. Topstep changed me.

THE BIGGEST LESSON TOPSTEP TAUGHT ME

At some point, you realize:

You don't trade to impress the market. You trade to protect your process.

The rules I once hated became the guardrails that kept my equity curve flat during losses and smooth during growth.

Topstep forced me to become:

- disciplined
- patient
- rule-based
- calm
- intentional
- mechanical

Topstep didn't give me funding. It gave me the boundaries that created the trader worthy of funding.

Freedom in trading doesn't come from breaking rules. It comes from mastering inside them.

Chapter 27 - The Multi-Account Strategy

(How to Multiply Income Without Multiplying Stress)

Scaling isn't about trading bigger.
Scaling is about trading smarter, cleaner, calmer — and with a structure that can be duplicated without falling apart.

Most traders fail when they try to scale because they try to scale emotion, not process.
They increase size, increase frequency, and increase pressure — and the system collapses.

My multi-account strategy is the opposite:

I scale *discipline*, not risk. **I duplicate *structure*, not stress.**

This is how prop-firm scaling becomes peaceful instead of chaotic.

THE CORE PHILOSOPHY

Scaling is NOT:

- "trade bigger"
- "win faster"
- "take more setups"

- "double the risk"

Scaling is:

- one setup
- one bracket
- one decision
- duplicated across multiple accounts
- with identical discipline

Once you understand this, multi-account trading becomes easy, mechanical, and shockingly predictable.

STEP 1 — ONE LEADER ACCOUNT

Everything begins with one master account, the "leader."

This account:

- chooses the setup
- sets the bracket
- follows all rules

- executes ONE clean trade per session
- determines whether followers trade or not

The leader account represents the highest version of your discipline.

Followers NEVER trade something the leader didn't trade.

Followers NEVER improvise.
Followers NEVER take extra setups.
Followers NEVER override.

If the leader doesn't trade → *everyone stands down.*

STEP 2 — THE FOLLOWER ACCOUNTS

Follower accounts are extensions of the leader's discipline.
They copy EXACTLY the same:

- entry levels
- stop-loss
- take-profit
- ATR confirmation

- volume confirmation
- ORB structure
- time cutoff
- one-trade rule

If the leader wins, followers win.
If the leader loses, followers lose — but with controlled, identical risk.

No follower ever risks more than the leader.

STEP 3 — RISK DISTRIBUTION (THE SAFE PYRAMID)

This is how I structure the family of accounts:

Leader Account (Funded)

- Risk: $250 per trade
- Purpose: Maintain cushion + long-term stability

Follower Accounts (Combines / Funded)

- Risk: $150–$200 per trade

- Purpose: Grow quietly, collect payouts, scale slowly

Each follower:

- stops trading for the week after reaching 1 TP
- pauses during drawdown
- follows leader without exception
- withdraws profits routinely

This keeps emotional pressure flat, even while accounts multiply.

STEP 4 — WEEKLY & MONTHLY RHYTHM

Every account follows the same professional structure:

Weekly Goal:

- $500 per account

Weekly Loss Cap:

- $300

Monthly Loss Cap:

- $600

This means:

- You never blow accounts
- You never spiral emotionally
- You never chase
- You never need “big weeks” to survive
- You compound quietly

Consistency becomes automatic.

STEP 5 — THE COPY ETHIC (THIS IS THE SECRET SAUCE)

Copy trading is not a shortcut.

It’s a responsibility.

If the leader breaks a rule →
every follower breaks a rule →
every account suffers →
scaling becomes chaos.

So before the leader takes any trade, I go through the Alignment Checklist:

✓ 4H trend aligned

✓ 1H trend aligned

✓ Clean 15m ORB

✓ ATR ≥ threshold

✓ Volume ≥ baseline

✓ VWAP distance clean

✓ One trade per session

✓ Cutoff respected

Only when ALL conditions are met do I take the trade — and EVERY follower copies it.

This is how one setup becomes five payouts.

STEP 6 — SCALING WITHOUT EGO

This is the part that destroys 90% of traders.

Scaling amplifies:

- ego
- impatience

- greed
- emotional pressure

Unless you remove ego from the equation completely.

My rule:

If a follower hits drawdown → PAUSE, don't panic.

If accounts stack profits → WITHDRAW, don't overtrade.

Each account is:

- data
- a sample
- a system check
- never a reflection of your worth

Over time:

- profits accumulate
- payouts stack
- pressure decreases
- discipline strengthens

- confidence becomes calm

Scaling becomes *peaceful* instead of stressful.

THE REAL TRUTH OF MULTI-ACCOUNT TRADING

It's not about making more money.

It's about proving to yourself:

"I can duplicate discipline."

When you can duplicate discipline:

- funding becomes effortless
- payouts become routine
- stress becomes minimal
- confidence becomes internal
- mastery becomes identity

Scaling is easy. Scaling discipline is the real skill.

And when you can do that, you become the trader you were meant to be.

Chapter 28- Journaling & Review System

(Where Growth Becomes Measurable)

If the market is your teacher, your journal is your truth.

Most traders avoid journaling because it exposes what they want to hide:

- impulses
- emotional trading
- broken rules
- hesitation
- revenge trades
- inconsistency

But the trader who avoids truth repeats the same mistakes forever.
The trader who records truth evolves faster than everyone else.

Your journal is not for statistics.
Your journal is for self-awareness —
because behavior repeats until it's recorded.

WHY JOURNALING MATTERS

Trading results are random in the short-term.
Trading behavior is NOT.

A clean journal reveals:

- why you really lost
- when you trade emotionally
- which sessions are strongest
- which sessions drain you
- whether ATR was too low
- whether you followed cutoff
- whether hesitation cost you

Some traders trade for years and never grow.
One trader journals for 30 days and sees exactly what needs to change.

Journaling exposes what discipline tries to hide.

THE SIX-COLUMN SYSTEM (THE ONE I USE)

A journal needs to be simple enough to maintain,
but detailed enough to produce clarity.

I use only six columns:

1. Session

(7 PM Globex, 2 AM London, 8:30 AM NY)

2. Setup

(ORB Long / ORB Short / Invalid Session)

3. ATR

(Volatility confirmation)

4. Emotion

(Calm / Hesitant / Anxious / Rushed)

5. Result

(+36 pts, –18 pts, BE, or 0 for skipped)

6. Notes

(One sentence only — the lesson of the session)

SAMPLE ENTRY (READY FOR YOUR BOOK)

Session	Setup	ATR	Emotion	Result
2 AM (London)	ORB Long	10.2	Calm	+36 pts

8:30 AM (NY)	ORB Short	9.4	Hesitant	−18 pts
7 PM (Globex)	No Trade	8.1	Neutral	0 pts

Nothing fancy. Nothing emotional.
Just data — clean, honest, repeatable.

THE WEEKLY REVIEW (THE REAL MAGIC)

Once a week, I spend 15–20 minutes answering four questions:

1. Did I follow every rule?

(One trade per session? ATR? Cutoff? ORB clean?)

2. What emotion repeated most?

(Calm = alignment. Hesitation = fear. Rushed = impatience.)

3. Which session produced the best results?

(Often London for structure, NY for volume.)

4. What ONE adjustment improves next week?

(Not five. Just ONE.)

This is how professionals evolve. Not by chasing more setups —
but by refining ONE behavior at a time.

EXPECTANCY — YOUR REAL EDGE

Most traders don't know if their system actually works.

Expectancy tells you the truth:

> Expectancy = (Win Rate × Average Win) – (Loss Rate × Average Loss)

If expectancy is positive, your system works —
you just need discipline.

If expectancy is negative, you don't have a trading problem —
you have a system problem.

Either way:

Your journal will show you exactly what's broken.

THE HIDDEN BENEFIT

Your journal becomes your confidence.

When you have proof of:

- your consistency
- your discipline
- your improvement
- your emotional growth
- your best sessions
- your best days
- your strongest conditions

you stop doubting yourself.

Confidence doesn't come from winning trades.
Confidence comes from consistent behavior recorded in your journal.

Your journal shows you who you are becoming —
and who you refuse to be again.

THE JOURNALING MANTRA

"Track behavior, not results —
because behavior is what creates results."

A trader without a journal is guessing.
A trader with a journal is growing.
And a trader who grows — wins.

Chapter 29 - The Breakeven Season

(The Plateau That Separates the Quitters from the Masters)

Every trader reaches a strange stage:

You're not losing anymore...
but you're not winning yet either.

Your equity curve goes flat.
Your emotions feel numb.
Your progress feels invisible.
And you start questioning everything.

This is The Breakeven Season —
the chapter almost nobody survives,
even though it is the single most important period in a trader's growth.

The irony?

Breakeven isn't stagnation.
It's stabilization.
It's the beginning of control.

It means your worst mistakes are gone:
- no more blowing accounts
- no more emotional spirals
- no more revenge trades
- no more overtrading
- no more gambling shots

Breakeven is the first sign you're trading like a professional.

WHAT BREAKEVEN REALLY MEANS

Breakeven feels like you're stuck, but it's the opposite.

It means:

- your losing streaks are shrinking
- your discipline is maturing
- your risk is stabilized
- your journal is showing patterns
- your bad habits no longer control you

Your equity is flat because you finally stopped damaging it.

Breakeven is healing.
Breakeven is repair.
Breakeven is foundation.

You cannot grow until you stop bleeding.
Breakeven is the first moment you've stopped the bleeding.

This is why most people quit right here:

They don't realize they're standing at the doorway to mastery.

THE MINDSET SHIFT THAT CHANGES EVERYTHING

During my own breakeven period, I shifted my thinking:
I stopped asking:

"How do I win more?"
and started asking:
"How do I lose less?"

This shift changed everything.

Winning takes care of itself when losing becomes controlled.

Breakeven taught me that trading mastery is:

- 80% defense
- 20% offense

And defense is built during this flat season.

If you're here now —
this is not the end of your progress. It is the beginning of your stability curve.

HOW TO SURVIVE THE BREAKEVEN SEASON

Here's what you must do now:

1. Trust your data, not your feelings.

If your journal shows rule consistency, you *are* improving.
Even if your account hasn't grown yet.

2. Stop changing your system.

Breakeven is a sign the system is stabilizing.
Tweaking everything resets your progress back to zero.

3. Accept boredom.

Boredom is a sign you're no longer being controlled by emotion.
This is a milestone — not a weakness.

4. Reduce pressure.

Breakeven means you're emotionally ready for consistency,
not financially ready for aggressive goals.

5. See this phase for what it is:

The turning point.

Every trader who becomes successful passes through this. It is the purification stage of discipline.

THE BREAKTHROUGH IS QUIET

One day, something unusual happens:

Your losses get smaller.
Your wins get cleaner.
Your emotions stay steady.
Your patience gets stronger.
And without realizing it...
your equity curve starts to lift.

Not because you're doing more —
but because you finally stopped doing too much.

Breakeven was never the plateau.
It was the runway.

CORE TRUTH OF THIS CHAPTER

Breakeven isn't failure.
It's proof you've stopped losing.
And when you stop losing —
winning becomes inevitable.

This is the moment where discipline solidifies,
and the curve of mastery quietly begins.

Chapter 30 - Turning Routine Into Mastery

(How Repetition Builds the Trader You Become)

Consistency isn't built in moments of inspiration —
it's built in the quiet routines nobody sees.

Most traders chase intensity:
big gains, big moments, big breakthroughs.

Professionals chase repetition.
They repeat the same process, the same rules, the same checklist, until their behavior becomes automatic.

Mastery isn't a skill. Mastery is a habit.

THE POWER OF DAILY RHYTHM

Your routine doesn't just support your trading —
it shapes your identity as a trader.

Just like an athlete warms up, a disciplined trader follows a ritual:

- same time
- same environment
- same checklist

- same setup
- same risk
- same review

This standardization removes emotion.
It removes chaos.
It removes decisions you shouldn't be making under pressure.

When your routine is automatic, your mind stays clear for the only thing that matters: execution.

THE 3 ROUTINES THAT GUARANTEE GROWTH

There are only three routines that matter in trading.
Master these, and your results follow naturally.

---

1. Pre-Session Routine — Identity Activation

Before you even open a chart, your mind must be aligned.

This routine includes:

- mood check

- sleep quality check
- emotional state check
- rule review
- ATR confirmation
- session cutoff reminder
- "one trade only" reminder

This is where you become the trader who trades well.

If the pre-session routine is sloppy, your trading will be sloppy too.

---

2. Execution Routine — Mechanical Precision

During the session, you follow a script — not your emotion.

- Clean ORB
- One direction bias
- No chasing
- No "quick scalps"

- Bracket set before entry
- Hands off
- Let the trade hit TP, SL, or be canceled

Execution must feel boring, because boredom means discipline is working.

---

3. Post-Session Routine — The Autopsy

This is where the real trader is built.

After every session, answer three questions:

1. Did I follow the process?

If yes → win. If no → lesson.

2. What emotion was present?

This becomes your psychology map.

3. What will I refine tomorrow?

One improvement. Not ten.

Mastery compounds like interest — slow at first, unstoppable later.

THE ROUTINE → IDENTITY CONNECTION

Here's the truth:

Your routine trains your mind.

Your mind trains your execution. Your execution trains your results.**

People think discipline creates routine. But it's actually routine that creates discipline.

Every structured session strengthens the identity:

"I am a trader who follows rules."
"I am a trader who executes cleanly."
"I am a trader who waits for alignment."

Identity drives behavior.
Behavior creates results.

REPETITION IS THE REAL MASTER

You don't rise to the level of your goals. You fall to the level of your habits.

A trader with poor habits will fail even with a perfect system.
A trader with strong habits will succeed even with an average system.

Success is built in these invisible repetitions.

What you repeat, you become. What you practice, you master.

THE MASTERY LOOP

Professional traders live inside a loop:

Routine → Execution → Review → Adjustment → Repeat

This loop builds:

- confidence
- consistency
- clarity
- emotional strength
- mechanical execution

Over time, your routine becomes your edge and your edge becomes your personality.

THE CORE TRUTH OF THIS CHAPTER

Mastery is not a moment. It's a rhythm.
A steady beat of repetition that shapes you into who you were meant to be.

When routine becomes identity, trading becomes natural — controlled, calm, and consistent.

Appendices

Reference Tools for Discipline and Execution

The following appendices are designed to support your trading journey with clarity and precision. These are not optional extras — they are the tools you return to repeatedly as your discipline matures and your system evolves.

Each appendix provides structure, data, or quick-reference material to help you maintain consistency across sessions, accounts, and market conditions.

These tools turn your process into something measurable, trackable, and scalable.

Appendix A

ATR-Adaptive Bracket Tables

(Your Volatility-Based Risk Framework)

ATR is the backbone of clean execution.
It tells you when the market has enough movement for your setup and when to stay out.
These tables are the exact volatility filters I use to avoid low-quality sessions and protect my discipline.

GOLD (MGC/XAU) — ATR (15-MIN) REQUIREMENTS

NY Session (8:30–10:30 AM)

- Minimum ATR(15m): 9+
- SL: 18 pts
- TP: 36 pts
- 1:2 Risk/Reward
- One trade per session only

London Session (2:00 AM)

- Minimum ATR(15m): 9+
- SL: 18 pts
- TP: 36 pts

Globex Session (7:00 PM)

- Minimum ATR(15m): 9+
- SL: 20 pts
- TP: 40 pts
- Slightly larger bracket due to slower movement during early evening

---

YM (DOW) — ATR (15-MIN) REQUIREMENTS

NY Session (8:30–10:30 AM)

- Minimum ATR(15m): 25+
- SL: 50 pts
- TP: 100 pts

London Session (2:00 AM)

- Minimum ATR(15m): 22–25+
- SL: 45–50 pts
- TP: 90–100 pts

Globex (7:00 PM)

- Minimum ATR(15m): 20+
- SL: 40 pts
- TP: 80 pts

HOW TO USE THIS TABLE

1. Check ATR before every session.

If ATR is under the threshold → SKIP.

2. Pre-set bracket based on the table.

Never adjust mid-trade.
Never widen your stop to "give it space."
Bracket is mechanical.

3. Let the session cancel your trade automatically.

If ORB doesn't trigger within your session cutoff, you are done.

4. Journal the ATR in every entry.

This builds pattern recognition over time.

WHY ATR SAVES TRADERS

Low ATR = choppy, indecisive markets
High ATR = clean, directional markets

ATR protects you from:

- boredom trades
- overtrading
- fake breakouts
- tight consolidations
- emotional impulses

This is your first line of defense.

Appendix B

Trade Journal Template

(The System That Keeps You Honest and Improving)

Your journal is the most important tool in your entire trading career.
This template is designed to be simple enough to maintain daily,
yet powerful enough to expose your behavior, patterns, and emotional tendencies.

Use this template *every session* — whether you traded or skipped.

THE SIX-COLUMN JOURNAL TEMPLATE

Below is the exact layout you can copy directly into Google Docs, Sheets, Notion, or any journaling software:

TRADE JOURNAL — DAILY ENTRY

Session	Setup	ATR (15m)	Emotion at Trigger
7 PM	ORB Long / ORB Short / No Trade	9.4	Calm / Hesitant / Anxious / Rushed
2 AM	ORB Long / ORB Short / No Trade	10.1	Calm
8:30 AM	ORB Long / ORB Short / No Trade	8.8	Nervous

Session	Result
7 PM	+36 / -18 / 0

2 AM	+36
8:30 AM	-18

INSTRUCTIONS FOR USE

1. Session

Identify which session you traded:

- 7 PM
- 2 AM
- 8:30–10:30 AM

2. Setup

Only one of these:

- ORB Long
- ORB Short
- No Trade (invalid session)

3. ATR

Record the ATR at the start of the 15m ORB.
Make sure it meets the required threshold.

4. Emotion at Trigger

Choose one:
Calm, Focused, Hesitant, Rushed, Anxious.

This builds emotional awareness over time.

5. Result

Record the raw points:
+36, -18, BE, or 0 for skipped.

6. Lesson

One sentence only.
Not a paragraph.
Not a story.
Just the *core takeaway*.

This forces clarity and growth.

WEEKLY REVIEW TEMPLATE

Every Friday or Saturday, complete these reflection questions:

1. Did I follow every rule this week?

List which ones were broken, if any.

2. Which session performed best for me?

Data will reveal your strongest window.

3. Which emotion repeated most often?

This becomes the focus for next week.

4. What's one improvement I bring into next week?

Not five. Just one.

This builds progressive refinement.

WHY THIS JOURNAL WORKS

This template trains:

- self-awareness
- consistency
- rule-following
- emotional regulation
- long-term discipline
- sample-size thinking

- data-driven adjustments

Your journal is the blueprint of your future equity curve.

What you track, you improve. What you ignore, repeats.

Appendix C

Prop-Firm Comparison Sheet

(Choosing the Right Firm for Your Style and Psychology)

Not all prop firms are created equal.
Some are built for speed.
Some are built for discipline.
Some are built for growth.

This comparison sheet breaks down the key differences so you can select the firm that best fits your system, personality, and long-term goals.

TOPSTEP — The Discipline Standard

Best For:

Traders who need structure, boundaries, and strict rules to reinforce discipline.

Strengths:

- Clear rules
- True behavioral evaluation
- Real funded accounts with consistency focus

- Strong risk parameters
- Best environment for long-term traders

Challenges:

- Tight daily loss limits
- No overtrading tolerance
- Requires emotional maturity

Ideal If You:

- Value routine
- Trade one setup
- Want real accountability
- Thrive under rules

APEX — The Scaling Machine

Best For:

Traders who want to scale multiple accounts aggressively.

Strengths:

- Frequent discounts
- Fast scaling
- Flexible rules
- Quick payouts

Challenges:

- More loopholes
- Less structure
- Easy to slip into bad habits

Ideal If You:

- Already have strong discipline
- Use an automated or mechanical system
- Want payouts fast and frequent

LEELoo — The Hybrid Option

Best For:

Traders who want strict rules but friendlier scaling.

Strengths:

- Good risk parameters
- Realistic drawdown
- Balanced evaluation
- Good customer support

Challenges:

- Less payout flexibility
- Slightly slower funding process

Ideal If You:

- Want structure
- But don't want extreme pressure
- And still want reliable payout windows

BULENOX — The Budget-Friendly Alternative

Best For:

Traders experimenting with prop firms for the first time.

Strengths:

- Low-cost evaluations
- Simple rules
- Frequent discounts

Challenges:

- Smaller brand
- Limited features
- Slower scaling options

Ideal If You:

- Are new to prop firms
- Want cheap testing
- Need to build early confidence

COMPARISON SUMMARY TABLE

Prop Firm	Best For	Strengths
Topstep	Discipline-focused traders	Structure, long-term growth
Apex	Fast scalers	High payout speed, flexible
Leeloo	Balanced traders	Realistic evaluations
Bulenox	Beginners or testers	Low cost

Prop Firm	Challenges	Emotional Profile
Topstep	Tight rules	Calm, consistent

Apex	Looser discipline required	Aggressive but controlled
Leeloo	Moderate scaling	Steady, rule-following
Bulenox	Slower growth	Learning phase

HOW TO CHOOSE THE RIGHT FIRM FOR YOU

1. What is your primary weakness?

- Impulse → Topstep
- Inconsistency → Leeloo
- Capital need → Apex
- Confidence building → Bulenox

2. What is your risk emotional profile?

- Calm and rule-based → Topstep
- Excited and aggressive → Apex
- Structured but adaptive → Leeloo

3. What is your long-term goal?

- Mastery → Topstep
- Payout stacking → Apex
- Balanced growth → Leeloo

THE TRUTH ABOUT PROP FIRMS

There is no "best" firm.
There is only the firm that makes YOU the best version of yourself.

Choose the one whose rules build your discipline, not the one whose shortcuts feed your impulses.

Appendix D

Session Behavior Cheat Sheet

(How Each Trading Window Behaves — And How to Trade It)

Every trading session has its own rhythm, personality, and tempo.
If you treat every session the same, you will trade out of sync with the market's natural flow.

This cheat sheet helps you instantly understand what to expect,
what setups are most reliable, and when you should avoid trading altogether.

---

7 PM — Globex Session

Personality: Slow, controlled, clean structure
Best For: Conservative ORB traders
Common Mistake: Entering too early due to boredom

Behavior Pattern:

- Low noise
- Tight structure

- Smooth breakouts
- Rare heavy volume
- Best for traders who value patience

What to Expect:

- Clean ORB shapes
- Few false breakouts
- Slightly larger brackets for safety
- More waiting, less action

Golden Rule:

If ATR < 9 for Gold or < 20 for YM → skip the session.

---

2 AM — London Session

Personality: Sharp, fast, precise
Best For: Traders who want movement without NY chaos
Common Mistake: Being surprised by volatility spikes

Behavior Pattern:

- Strong momentum
- Deep candle wicks
- Quick directional commitment
- ORB often triggers cleanly

What to Expect:

- Fast triggers
- High-quality breakouts
- Better volume than Globex
- Smaller SL hits if structure is clean

Golden Rule:

Expect sudden reversals — take the first clean ORB only.

8:30–10:30 AM — New York Session

Personality: Volatile, emotional, high-energy
Best For: Traders with strong discipline
Common Mistake: Overtrading after a win or loss

Behavior Pattern:

- Heavy volume
- Explosive moves
- News-driven spikes
- ORB structure forms fast

What to Expect:

- The cleanest volume confirmations
- Biggest wins
- Biggest losses if emotional
- Most impulsive mistakes

Golden Rule:

Never trade past 10:30 AM — volatility shifts into randomness.

SESSION COMPARISON TABLE

Session	Tempo	Risk Level	Volume Pattern
7 PM Globex	Slow	Low	Light
2 AM London	Fast	Medium	Strong
NY Session	High Energy	High	Explosive

Session	Best Skill Required
7 PM Globex	Patience
2 AM London	Precision
NY Session	Emotional Control

WHEN TO SKIP A SESSION

Skip instantly if any of the following are true:

- ATR below threshold
- ORB structure overlapping

- Volume baseline weak
- Emotional state negative
- Personal life distractions
- You feel rushed or tired

Skipping is not missing opportunity.
Skipping is **preserving consistency.**

SESSION STRENGTH RANKING (Based on Clean ORB Behavior)

1. **London (2 AM)** — best structure + best movement
2. **Globex (7 PM)** — cleanest ORB, slow but controlled
3. **New York** — highest volume, highest emotional risk

Each session has its place —
your job is to match your behavior to the session's personality.

THE CORE TRUTH OF THIS APPENDIX

Sessions are not random.
They are predictable rhythms.
Learn the rhythm, and execution becomes effortless.

Closing Message

The Trader You're Becoming

(A Reflection on Patience, Process, and Identity)

If you are holding this book in your hands, you're already different from most traders.

Most people chase setups.
Most people chase indicators.
Most people chase shortcuts.

But you chose to build:

- patience
- structure
- discipline
- emotional control
- mastery
- a mindset that can weather anything

That alone puts you in the top 1%.

Trading is not about charts.
It's not about entries or exits.
It's not even about money.

Trading is the mirror that shows you exactly who you are.

It exposes impatience.
It magnifies fear.
It amplifies doubt.
It confronts ego.
It demands honesty.

But it also rewards the trader who is willing to evolve.

THE TRADER WHO FINISHES THIS BOOK IS NOT THE SAME AS THE ONE WHO STARTED IT

You now understand:

- how shortcuts destroy growth
- how patience compounds
- how discipline protects your future
- how to trade inside structure
- how to wait for alignment
- how to execute calmly
- how to scale responsibly

- how to journal intelligently
- how to treat trading like a profession

This isn't theory. This is transformation.

A silent, internal transformation —
the kind that turns a person into a professional.

YOUR NEXT CHAPTER ISN'T IN THIS BOOK — IT'S IN YOUR ROUTINE

From this point forward, your power will come from:

- consistency
- repetition
- controlled risk
- emotional awareness
- reinforcement of the routines outlined here

There will be slow seasons.
There will be breakeven periods.
There will be flat curves.
There will be setbacks.

But you now know:

Those are not signs of failure.
They are the signs of mastery forming beneath the surface.

You're not just learning how to trade.
You're learning how to stay in the game long enough to win.

A MESSAGE FROM ME TO YOU

Life didn't make this journey easy for me.
I fought battles in silence.
I lost money alone.
I traded through isolation.
I questioned myself more times than I can count.

But patience rewarded me.
Discipline rebuilt me.
Trading matured me.
And now — mastery is shaping me.

If my journey can help even one trader avoid quitting, then every loss, every setback, every painful lesson was worth it.

MY FINAL WORDS TO YOU

If you stay patient, protect your process, and honor your structure —

you *will* succeed.
Not because the market favors you, but because mastery rewards patience.

Your breakthrough will come.
Your equity curve will rise.
Your discipline will hold.
Your identity will sharpen.
Your confidence will stabilize.

And you will become the trader
you always knew you could be.

About the Author

Joël Pérodin

(Art, Discipline, and a Seven-Year Journey Through Trading)

Joël Pérodin is an entrepreneur, photographer, music producer, and trader based in the Washington, D.C. metropolitan area. His journey into trading didn't begin with a dream of fast money — it began with curiosity. He wanted to understand why the market intimidated so many people, why most traders quit, and why consistency seemed so rare.

Over seven years of relentless learning, Joël discovered that trading wasn't a battle against charts — it was a battle against himself.
He burned through more than thousands in pursuit of clarity, fought through isolation, and learned the hard truth:
you don't trade the market — you trade your psychology.

Joël's trading philosophy blends structure with self-awareness, creativity with discipline, and simplicity with precision. He believes that mastery is less about predicting the market and more about mastering the rhythms within ourselves — the impulses, emotions, and habits that shape every decision.

His mission is simple:
help traders stay in the game long enough to win.

Whether through art, entrepreneurship, or trading, Joël carries the same message across every discipline:

"Mastery rewards patience."

Contact & Reader Invitation

Connect With Me

(For Questions, Guidance, or Hands-On Mentorship)

If this book spoke to you, helped you, or opened your eyes to the deeper side of trading, I want you to know something:

You don't have to walk this journey alone.

I spent years fighting my battles in silence — losing money quietly, learning lessons the hard way, and growing without anyone to talk to who truly understood the psychological side of this craft. I don't want you to go through that alone.

If you have questions about:

- trading psychology
- the ORB method
- prop-firm structure
- discipline and routine
- emotional control
- or even your own struggles and doubts

I invite you to reach out to me directly.

🖂 Email:

jperenterprises@gmail.com

I read every message myself.
And I respond to every person who reaches out.

Whether you're a beginner, stuck in the breakeven season, or on the edge of your breakthrough, I'm here to support you the way I wish someone had supported me during my early years.

Thank you for reading.
Thank you for growing.
Thank you for staying in the game.

Your journey matters — and I'm honored to be a part of it.

Mastery rewards the ones who refuse to quit.
And you made it all the way to the last page.

This isn't the end.
It's the beginning of the trader you're becoming.

www.ingramcontent.com/pod-product-compliance
Lightning Source LLC
LaVergne TN
LVHW100311210926
848480LV00003B/1088

* 9 7 9 8 2 9 5 4 1 5 2 9 6 *